Anger Overload in Children:

Additional Strategies for Teachers and Parents

Volume 2

By David Gottlieb, Ph.D.

Volume 1 (published in 2012) is
Anger Overload in Children: A Parent's Manual

Anger Overload in Children: Additional Strategies for Teachers and Parents

Table of Contents

Acknowledgements

I'd like to thank the families that I have worked with in my office and those who have e-mailed me over the years for their feedback on the strategies I have developed.

My wife Fawn has patiently read over this manuscript several times and helped make my writing clearer. Thanks also to Lev, Shira, and Seth for their input. I have also talked over some of the strategies with clinicians in my office, and I thank you all for your feedback.

David Gottlieb, Ph.D.
February 2015

Other books by Dr. David Gottlieb:

Anger Overload in Children: A Parent's Manual

Your Child is Defiant: Why is Nothing Working?

Why Is My Child's ADHD Not Better Yet? Recognizing Undiagnosed Secondary Conditions That May Be Affecting Your Child's Treatment (with co-authors Thomas Shoaf and Risa Graff)

Introduction

Over the last few years since my parent's manual Anger Overload in Children was published, I have received several hundred stories and questions from parents and teachers. In this supplement to my manual, I provide answers to some of the questions I have received. I will introduce additional strategies for the home and show how many of the strategies can be adapted for school.

For children who are quick to anger, often one of the underlying problems is that they expect something of themselves or of others that is unrealistic or that is very unlikely to happen. There is increased risk that these children will become disappointed and have an angry explosion then. These children are genuinely surprised when their expectations are not met, and they become enraged. The problem is that their expectations are unrealistic, or in some way based on a false premise.

The theme running through many of the chapters in this supplement to my manual is how to help these children learn to keep perspective. If they have realistic expectations, their anger is less likely to be triggered. I will present techniques that parents and teachers can use to help these children. For the first time, I have included a section especially for teachers.

I have organized the chapters in this book into five sections. The first section of this update dovetails with the first part of my parent's manual. In both my parent's manual and this update, I first discuss strategies that parents can use without the direct participation of their child. In my update I focus on how to help children who are sensitive to criticism. Some children are easily hurt by relatively minor negative remarks, or get extremely upset when they make mistakes in school. If your child is sensitive to criticism or mistakes and also quick to erupt in anger, what should you do? One approach I have found to be very effective is to use "mantras" (short memorable sayings). I explain how to come up with useful mantras for your child. Often these sayings can help a child keep perspective. If you can help a child see things in a new way, you can head off anger overload before it starts!

The next chapter re-visits a subject that parents have frequently asked about: when to use rewards and when to use negative consequences. These can be difficult to apply effectively with children prone to anger overload. Sometimes incentives (i.e. rewards) and consequences can help motivate a child to use new strategies to prevent or limit angry outbursts. But before you try incentives or consequences, be sure to work with your child on a strategy for managing frustration, because if a child has not begun to master a strategy, then incentives and consequences may cause more frustration and precipitate anger overload

In part two of this supplement, just like in my parent's manual, I turn to cognitive strategies that parents can teach their children. The first chapter in this section explains how to determine if your child is ready to learn cognitive strategies. The next chapter is about how to motivate your child to work together with you on these strategies. The third and last chapter in this section explains what to do for young children, under the age of seven, who are usually too young to work on cognitive strategies. You can use imaginary stories as a way to "seed" new ideas on handling anger. In the stories you create, your child's hero learns to control his anger. Your child will "indirectly" learn how to have self-control by hearing what his hero does.

The third section of the update answers questions about common triggers of anger overload: meal time, teasing, and violent cartoons and video games. I discuss what parents can do in these situations to head off tantrums. At family events like dinnertime, it can be trying on everyone else when one child has a tantrum. I generally recommend parents ignore tantrums, but what if the rest of the family is affected by a child's intense screaming at the dinner table. What else can you do?

Some children explode when they are teased by their peers in school. I explain how parents and teachers can help these children learn not to react so strongly to being teased. Another trigger can be violent video games. Children can get very stirred up playing these games, and they may start screaming or throwing things when they inevitably lose. Should parents restrict the use of these games? And will violent television shows and movies lead to more violent outbursts by your child?

The next to last section of this update is especially for teachers. While my parent's manual focuses on what parents can do at home, I wanted in this update to give teachers suggestions on how to apply the strategies in school. It can be more difficult to manage an outburst in a room full of students. What works, and what does not work, in a classroom?

Finally, I write about how to find professional help. If you are having problems implementing the strategies, how do you go about finding the right mental health professional to help your child and your family?

These are among some of the issues I will address in this update to my anger overload manual. Hundreds of parents have written to me for help with their child's problems and if you want to read some of these e-mails, check out my blog online: yourchildisdefiant.blogspot.com. Many parents have found it helpful to read what others are going through with their children, so I recommend you take a look at the blog. It will help to see that you are not alone.

At the end of this update, I include extra copies of worksheets you can use when working on some of the strategies I describe in this book. It takes time and practice to help a child with anger overload issues. Use the worksheets to help organize your thinking and plan your approach.

Anger overload is not included as a diagnosis in and of itself in the current diagnostic manual published by the American Psychiatric Association. Anger is viewed as a part of other diagnoses, but the problem with this approach is that many children have frequent angry outbursts but do not have the features of other disorders. An angry child is not usually bipolar, depressed, nor oppositional. I think the reason anger overload is not included in the psychiatric association's diagnostic manual as a stand alone diagnosis is that it is hard to decide at what point angry outbursts become serious enough to be classified as a "disorder."

In my view, it is less important where the dividing line is and more important that parents are provided with strategies to help their children develop better self-control. Anger overload is a real problem for many children, and there are numerous biological studies that suggest there can be miscommunication between the emotional structures of the brain, specifically the amygdala, and the rational structures of the brain, specifically the prefrontal cortex, when anger gets out of hand.

Some children will mature on their own and learn to handle anger, but many benefit from strategies parents can employ to help their children develop better self-control. Everything we do is dependent on our brains, and the more we practice a new skill, the quicker our brains change and adapt. While for many children it takes months or years to develop better self-control, it is worth the effort. In order to have good relationships with other people and to be successful at work and play, it is important to learn how to handle anger. So hang in there. Your work with your child is well worth the effort.

David Gottlieb, Ph.D.

Part I: Parents as the Agent of Change

Helping Sensitive Children Keep Perspective

Some children get their feelings hurt easily when things do not go the way they expected. This can happen when they make a mistake, or when they lose a game, or when they are mildly rebuked. While some of these children internalize their pain, those children who are prone to intense angry feelings can have frequent angry explosions when they feel "injured." You can see this in many examples (sent in by parents) on my blog: yourchildisdefiant.blogspot.com.

For these children there are additional techniques that are helpful in heading off an outburst. The first is to help them "**put it in perspective**." For example, if a child feels criticized when you tell him to fix something in his homework, or if he feels angry when he loses a video game, you would say something **before** you talk about the homework, or **before** he plays the video game, that would help him keep perspective. You would point out what he does well before any problems occur. For the homework, after you have looked it over, you could say "Hey, you've done a good job on this, but I think you made a small mistake on this one." Or for the video game, before your child starts playing, you could say "You are good at this game but remember the game makers design the game to be difficult on purpose so that you can't win all the time. When you play this game, remember they are going to make it so you lose eventually."

Notice that it is important to say these words before your child starts the activity that in the past has triggered his rage, or in the case of homework, before you point out any mistakes. Once a child is upset, the words intended to help your child keep perspective will have little effect. When emotional, children with anger overload are not usually thinking rationally about their behavior. But before a child gets emotional, cues that help him keep perspective can be helpful. The goal is to provide his rational brain an idea that can help before emotion interferes.

Now this will not always work. Your child may forget what you said by the time he gets upset. Or he may not pay attention to your cue to keep perspective. But if you use these words repeatedly over the next few months in situations that have caused your child to feel hurt, eventually the cue words will begin to help prevent an outburst. Remember to stay calm yourself throughout this process. Do not get angry if your child ignores your help and has an explosion. And do not criticize him for not listening to you.

When the "triggering" activity is about to start again another day, then use your cue words again. You can also heighten the effect by preparing in advance pictures or songs to help make the cues more meaningful and more memorable. If your child likes to draw, see if he can make a picture that illustrates a more balanced view of himself. For example, for the situation when a child makes a mistake on his homework, suggest he draw what it feels like to get most everything right even if there are a few mistakes. You want the picture to focus on the new perspective you want your child to take. Hang the picture wherever your child typically does his homework.

Or together with your child make up a jingle, or saying, that helps him keep perspective when doing homework: "I get most of them right." Or "mistakes are normal." Or "everyone gets some wrong." Or "no one is perfect." The idea is to come up with a memorable phrase that your child chooses with you. If your child helps to pick out the phrase then he is more likely to use it. For some children, their memory for the phrase will be aided if it is set to music--like a jingle for a product advertised on television. Each time your child is starting the activity where he has lost perspective in the past, sing the jingle for him, and have him join you if he is not too self-conscious. Eventually, after a number of months, your child may hear the jingle in his head without you having to sing it to him.

Also do not forget to use yourself as a role model. If you have made an error at work or in some leisure activity, talk with your child about it before he begins a difficult task. Mention how you felt bad, and what you tried to do to keep from exploding. In this way, you are showing your child that he is not alone. Not only are you normalizing the hurt he feels when he makes a mistake, but you are modeling one possible way to deal with it.

If your child is repeatedly making many mistakes on his homework, then you need to talk with his teacher and try to find out why. It is not enough to try to soothe your child's feelings. Cues like "everyone makes mistakes sometimes" would not be useful if your child cannot do most of his homework. The problem is different than for the child who explodes when he makes a few errors. There is something else going on. The problem could be that your child a) is not motivated, or b) has trouble concentrating, or c) has a learning problem. If the teacher is not sure what might be happening, ask if the school can do an evaluation of your child's cognitive skills and emotional state. Usually this involves testing by the school psychologist. Then you can ask the school to help develop a plan so that your child will succeed.

Worksheet for Helping Sensitive Children

What trigger will you help your child deal with?

_____

What will be the cue to help your child keep perspective?

_____

Will you use a picture, song, or jingle to help reinforce the cue words?

_____

Is there an example from your own life you can mention as a model for your child?

_____

What is a Mantra and When To Use It

In my parent's manual, I suggest teaching a child to use mantras as a cognitive strategy to help the child think before reacting. However, many children are not ready to learn to use a mantra on their own to head off an outburst. If a child has not acknowledged he has a problem or is not willing to work on it, he will not see the value in learning a mantra. Still, parents and teachers can use mantras as "cues" to help children keep perspective. It is not necessary to teach it to the child in order for the mantra to be useful in helping to head off a tantrum.

This approach is similar to what I just suggested you do for sensitive children. The same technique is useful for other triggers of anger, such as an unexpected change in the family's weekend schedule. Let's say you planned on going to a movie with your family, but in the morning one of your children is sick, and you need to stay home. You could let your other child know hours before you would have gone to the movie that his sibling is ill, and that you will re-schedule the movie for next weekend. You could use a mantra like "crap happens" (if this word is not prohibited in your house). This will work if your child is amused by your choice of words. If you can change your child's emotional state from frustration to amusement, then he will be much less likely to explode. Then you could suggest a fun activity he could do at home: maybe he could help you pick out a movie to watch at home.

Other examples of phrases that could help a child keep perspective are: "Let's think how we can turn lemons into lemonade," or "Let's turn this rotten egg into a golden egg," "Let's make the clouds go away, and turn this into a sunny day." In these examples, the message is "we can still have fun if we think of a new plan." Suggest that you think together about what you could do at home that is fun since you can't go out and leave his sick sibling home alone. While the approach in the previous paragraph was to inject humor, the tactic here is to inspire your child to think of alternatives and not to give up on having fun. In both cases you are altering your child's feelings of disappointment. If you can get your child either to laugh or to feel hopeful, you will prevent his initial frustration from escalating into a tantrum.

To summarize, the mantra is a short memorable saying that helps your child maintain a positive mood. If you have observed a type of situation that tends to cause your child frustration, you could work with your child ahead of time to come up with a mantra that your child finds amusing or interesting.

When you are working through the first half of the manual and implementing strategies that do not involve your child's direct participation, use mantras as an additional strategy in your "toolbox." Try coming up with a saying or jingle that might help your child keep perspective before he reaches the overload phase. The saying may not help every time. But if sometimes you can get your child's attention with the jingle before he gets too angry, it may help him stay calm.

Remember that in order for your child to pay attention to the mantra, the saying must be catchy in some way. It might have a bit of humor, or use words that the child thinks are cool. If the mantra does not grab your child, it won't likely help. For example, you could use the phrase "everyone makes mistakes" to help a child deal with making mistakes in school or in a video game at home. However, that phrase may not resonate with your child. But if you change the words to "even Batman (or some superhero he admires) makes mistakes," he may pay more attention. Also consider using words that your child thinks are forbidden or unusual. For example, one child I worked with smiled when we came up with the cue words: "sometimes crap happens." The child's smile was a signal that this phrase had power to help him. His smiling indicated that his mood had softened, that the phrase had "touched" him. Don't be afraid to be silly or even gross in your choice of words. You want a saying that your child will find appealing and catchy.

When To Use Incentives and Consequences:

Sometimes children respond to brief and immediate incentives or negative consequences, and you can try to use them to reinforce a new coping strategy to deal with anger. Whether you want to encourage your child to use a calming strategy (from the first half of the manual) or to use a cognitive approach (from the second half of the manual), there are a few important points to keep in mind if you are going to try adding incentives or consequences:

First, before you introduce any incentives or consequences, decide what new coping strategy you want to work on with your child and begin practicing it with your child for a couple of weeks. The strategy may come from the first half of the manual, such as developing a relaxation space in your house, or come from the second half of the manual, such as teaching your child catch phrases to help him stay calm. Practice the new strategy when your child is not upset, and then in about two weeks, tell him/her you are proud of him and that the next time he feels frustrated you will remind him to try it.

Now you can also introduce the idea of incentives. (Another word for incentives is rewards.) Talk together about some brief incentives and tell him that he can choose one if he attempts the new strategy. Notice that your child would get to pick one of several rewards that you both agreed on. It is more fun if you don't use just one reward all the time.

Your child earns the reward *if he tries*. It will be hard for him to control his anger and you don't want to focus on success, but on effort.

Try to help him "catch" the frustration in the early stages. You can use cue words that remind him of the new coping strategy. It is at this early stage of anger that your child's rational brain will be most engaged, and it is at this time that your child has the best chance of controlling his anger. If he responds to your cues and tries to calm himself, praise him and ask him to pick a reward.

I would not recommend using consequences until your child has had some success with the new strategy, and has been able to reduce the frequency of outbursts. You want your child to have some calming tools in place before you use negative consequences. If he has not learned any calming skills yet, a negative consequence is not going to help and will likely make him even more frustrated.

Usually a child has to experience the negative consequence one or more times, so that the memory of the consequence might be on his mind the next time he starts to get angry. The key words in the previous sentence are "on his mind the next time he starts to get angry." A child is still thinking rationally in the early phases of frustration, but once he hits anger overload, his ability to reason is overwhelmed by his strong emotion. Once in overload, it is unlikely he will think about consequences.

If you want to try using a consequence, pick a short term one, like no computer time after dinner. Furthermore, be very clear about exactly what behavior would bring about that consequence (for example, your child may be using swear words that you want stopped).

Keep in mind that the consequence has to be something meaningful to your child, and sometimes you don't know what will motivate him until you try something. And do not talk about the consequence while your child is in anger overload. Just prepare him ahead of time when everyone is calm about what is expected if he wants to avoid a consequence. When he gets angry, if he does not try a coping strategy or if he uses words that you have explained are inappropriate, then impose the consequence once he has calmed down. Mention it in a matter of fact way without a lot of emotion or a lot of discussion.

Be sure also to praise your child (Praise is essentially a verbal reward.) whenever he tries a strategy. If consequences cause more outbursts, then hold off in the future on these consequences, and go back to the other approaches in my parent's manual.

In actuality, if you follow the guide in my manual, you are using *natural* incentives and consequences without having to impose extra negative consequences! Specifically, you are paying attention (which is rewarding) to your child when he is working with you on self-control strategies, and you are ignoring (negative consequence) when he is in the anger overload phase.

One last point about using rewards and consequences: They work best when both parents agree on the plan, and both implement the plan. In two parent families, if one parent does not support the use of rewards or consequences, they are less likely to be effective. Your child will sense that one parent is hesitant and will try to get that parent to change the plan. If you both do not agree on some part of the plan, then leave that part out. Start with what you can agree on, and see how that goes. There is a better chance then that your child will take seriously a plan that is endorsed by both of you, and your child is more likely then to try to earn the rewards and avoid the consequences.

Worksheet for Incentives and Consequences

Which anger trigger will you be working on? _____

What coping strategy do you want your child to try?

_____

What cue words will you use to remind him if he starts to get frustrated?

_____

What incentives can your child choose from if he tries?

_____

What specific behavior will lead to a negative consequence?

_____

What will be the brief negative consequence?

_____

Part II: Teaching Your Child New Skills

When is Your Child Ready To Learn Cognitive Strategies

Not every child is ready for the cognitive strategies in the second half of my parent's manual. On average, between the ages of seven and nine, children recognize that they have become angry and can talk at least somewhat about their anger after they have calmed down. Often younger children below the age of seven or eight have difficulty with **self-monitoring**, that is, recognizing and "owning" their angry behaviors. This is necessary to work together with you or a therapist on the cognitive strategies in the second half of the manual. "Owning" means accepting responsibility for one's behavior. Young children sometimes do not think they did anything excessive or wrong. They tend to blame other people entirely. So if a child does not realize that he is having outbursts, or if he realizes he is getting angry but blames it all on others, he will not be ready to work on cognitive strategies, such as labeling different levels of anger or looking at points of view other than his own. But if he can take at least some responsibility for his outbursts, then I would recommend you try to teach your child cognitive approaches to controlling anger.

It is not only young children who may not be ready to work on the strategies in the second half of the manual. Older children sometimes have trouble with these strategies too. In that case, you would stick with the strategies in the first half of the manual because these do not require the child's direct participation.

Another skill that is necessary for your child to be able to work with you on cognitive approaches to anger is the ability to put what one is feeling into words. Describing one's emotions is more abstract than talking about what you ate for dinner! You can help your child describe his feelings by giving him a few choices and asking if one of the choices is what he felt. Or you can ask him to draw a picture of how he felt. If your child is struggling to talk about his behavior and feelings, keep the discussion brief and come back to it another day.

Here is what I recommend you start with if you want to work on the cognitive strategies in the second half of the manual. First try to develop a cooperative discussion with your child about anger. I write in more detail in the next chapter about how to engage your child in the process. You want your child to feel like this is going to be a joint venture and that you are not going to be critical. You realize anger can be tough to control. If possible, mention an example where you had trouble controlling your anger, so your child won't feel singled out.

Then, a good first cognitive strategy to work on is observing different levels of anger. See if your child can identify how he acts when he is a little angry compared to when he is very angry. You could label different degrees of anger with neutral words, like colors. Red could be for extreme anger, yellow for medium levels of anger, and blue for lower amounts of anger. I explain how to implement this strategy in more detail in my parent's manual. The goal is for a child to begin to recognize the difference between how he reacts when he is a little frustrated compared with how he reacts when he is in anger overload. Once he can identify early stages of anger, he may be able to work with you on cognitive coping strategies that can head off more explosive anger.

David Gottlieb, Ph.D.

How To Motivate Your Child

Before you begin working with your child on the cognitive strategies in the second half of the manual, an important first step is to build a "working alliance" with him/her. That means you want your child to be engaged in the process: it is important that this be a cooperative project. How do you elicit your child's participation in working on his anger? After all, this is going to be difficult for him since his anger gets triggered easily.

A very important first step is to communicate empathy. You want your child to know that it is not easy to control anger and that you understand that. Explain that everyone gets angry, and some people get angry in a short time: they are "quick reactors." You would mention that you think your child is a quick reactor. You could add that because anger can come on so quickly, it can be hard to control. You therefore do not expect immediate changes, you just want to start to work on it together.

And you will not get mad if your child cannot control it right away. By saying this, you are communicating that you want to be helpful, and that you will not be critical, because this is hard work. Mention to him that if he should feel you are getting upset with him as you work on anger issues, he should tell you right away, and you will try to stay calm and non-judgmental.

At this point, you want to draw a connection with other people in the family who can get very angry in a short period of time. Better yet, if you can think of a time you were angry, use yourself as an example. You could also say how hard it was (or is) for you to work on it. You want your child to feel that he is not alone!

Also you can explain that there is no one right way to express anger. It is a powerful emotion, and different people have different ways of expressing it. If possible, give a few examples of how you and/or he have expressed anger over the last few weeks. Then add that you will try to work with him on figuring out alternatives that do not hurt people's feelings too much, that do not verbally or physically harm people or people's possessions.

Over the next few weeks, you want to review for a few minutes each night what you and/or he have become angry about that day. I suggest you write some notes on a chart or on the computer so that you have a written record to look back at in the future. You can use chart #1 entitled "Recording angry interactions" from my parent's manual, or make your own chart. Basically, you want to record what was happening at the time, and what each person said leading up to the angry outburst. This should be done in a non-judgmental way and should not take more than five minutes. Praise your child for whatever effort he makes to remember what happened that day. If he can't think of anything, but you remember an incident, you would mention it and ask what got him mad. Make a note of what he said, even if it is not exactly the way you or your spouse see it. You want him to feel you take his ideas seriously. If your child would not feel criticized if your input is a little different than his, you could add your observations to his on the

17

chart. Make sure you communicate that both your ideas make sense. In most cases, the parent is the note taker, unless your child asks to do it. Some nights there may be nothing to record and that is okay.

The idea of the record keeping is to help everyone begin to see patterns, or what I call themes. There will not be an obvious trigger for every outburst, but you want to see if there are any common themes. After a few weeks, look over the incidents together and point out one possible theme for some of the angry outbursts. Children usually have difficulty finding themes themselves, and this is why I recommend you point out a theme to your child. Use words that are non-critical. Say that you will soon begin working with him on how else he could handle that type of situation.

Now you are ready to begin working on the strategies in the second half of the manual. You have set the tone that this is a cooperative effort. It is more likely that your child will work with you on the difficult process of learning new strategies if your child feels that his ideas are being taken seriously and if he does not feel you are criticizing him.

Using Imagination and Play with Young Children

If you have implemented the strategies in the first half of my original parent's manual, and you try to start working on the cognitive strategies in the second half of the manual, but your child does not want to acknowledge or talk about his anger with you, then you could try using a more indirect approach for now. This is especially helpful for younger children who are often not yet aware of their emotional states or who are not ready to take responsibility for their angry behavior. These children shut down when you try to talk with them about their behavior. Or they consistently blame other people for causing their outbursts. The strategies in the second half of the manual are helpful for children who 1) have the ability to look at their behavior once they have calmed down, and 2) wish they could control their anger better. If your child is not ready for the strategies in part two of the manual, there are alternative ways to engage your child, once you have finished part one of the manual.

What I would recommend is that instead of having a direct discussion with your child about his anger, you use fictional stories and imaginary play. The stories you make up with your child would be about cartoon figures your child watches on television, or about his/her favorite stuffed animals, or about superheroes your child admires. You can either make up the story yourself, or start a story and ask your child to help you add to it. Then you would tell it at night when your child is in bed, or at any relatively quiet family time, e.g. in the car or in the bath. If you want, you can act out the stories with puppets or toy figures you have at home. Sometimes this makes the stories more memorable. Either way, you would do this several nights a week over the next few months. You would vary the stories once your child seems to be getting bored. The goal is to begin an indirect discussion of anger by using fictional characters.

Before you start, think about what themes you want the story to contain. Use themes that are consistent with your child's triggers, and write stories and resolutions that are dramatic. In other words, if your child's trigger is putting his toys away, the story might be about a fictional character playing with toys. But if this content is not dramatic enough to interest your child, then change the topic to something more exciting and dramatic. For example, the character could be flying through space and playing ball with the clouds, when his mother sends him a message in a flying rocket that it is bedtime. The character in the story does not want to stop and gets so angry he screams loudly. His breath is so powerful that the clouds all blow away. Then he begins to cry because all the clouds have left. His mother hears him crying and comes flying into the sky. She hugs him and tells him not to worry, that it is late and the clouds went to bed, but they will come around again tomorrow. The mother in the story would add a helpful hint: "Maybe next time, blow kisses, or say see you tomorrow, when it is time to say goodbye to the clouds." You want the story to be appealing and send a message, but it needs to be indirect for your child to be interested and listen. It is about a space creature and the clouds, not about your child!

Another example of a story about anger getting out of control could be about an imaginary giant who is playing with giant boulders when his sister comes by and calls him a weakling. He gets furious and throws giant boulders at his sister. His sister jumps out of the way, and the boulders almost land on a house. Then a wise superhero says "you might destroy their house throwing the boulders around like that. Why don't you build a fort with the boulders instead. Then you can play inside the fort and your sister won't see you." You want the theme of the story to relate to your child's troubles with anger, and also you want the characters and action in the story to be appealing to your child. Practice telling stories with your spouse, and when you are ready, try it one night with your child.

The two vignettes above are about anger that gets out of control, and both have endings that speak to alternative behaviors that are less destructive and more pro-social. If your child tends to get into arguments with other people, you could make up a story where two characters are at odds with each other, but learn to make peace. You might include a wise old woman who says that "Talking works when you don't scream." You are seeding ideas about self-control in these stories. But at the same time you do not directly mention your child or his problems controlling anger.

Other ideas would be to make up a funny song with lyrics about anger that has a helpful resolution, or make pictures together about anger, or read together a story book about anger. You could ask a children's librarian for suggestions of children's books about anger or look online. Again, the basic idea is to begin a "discussion" about anger indirectly with your young child.

Also, be sure to use yourselves as an example in some of your discussions. While you don't yet talk about your child's anger, it is a good idea to begin talking about how you have handled anger, even if you are not always proud of how you acted. You are trying to normalize the idea that people get angry, and at the same time, by talking about your approach to anger, you are using it as an example for your child to emulate. If you recently got angry at work, talk out loud at dinner about what happened to cause you to get angry, and say how you handled it. If you acted in a way that you don't want your child to emulate, then change the ending a little bit, but don't make yourself sound perfect.

All these techniques give the message to your child that everyone gets angry and that it is okay to talk about it. It may be a year or more before your child is ready to talk more directly about his anger. In the meantime, continue to try to engage your child with stories or songs for a few minutes at bedtime several nights each week.

After a few months, ask him if he ever felt like the character in the story. Gently begin a discussion, and empathize with what bothered him. Some days later you could wonder out loud if he has felt that way again (do not do this while he is in the midst of an outburst, but maybe later that night) and suggest that he could be like the superhero in the story you were telling at bedtime, assuming the superhero had figured out a more adaptive way to deal with his anger. If your child accepts that he felt angry similar to the characters in your story, then he is ready to begin the second half of the manual. If not, then stick with the story telling for another few months, along with the other strategies in the first half of the manual. Then try again to begin a discussion about your child's anger. This may seem like a lot of work, and it is. But it is well worth the effort in the long run! If your child learns to deal with his anger in a more pro-social way, it will help him have better relationships in the family, at school, and later as an adult.

Worksheet for Creating Stories and Jingles

What trigger will you focus on?

_____

What characters and activity in your story will capture the trigger in a dramatic way?

_____

Will you use puppets or toy figures to tell your story?

_____

Will you use a jingle or song?

_____

What alternative behavior(s) do you wish your child would use?

_____

How will you resolve your story in a way that suggests an alternative?

_____

Part III: How To Handle Some Common Triggers

Meal Time and Family Activities

A frequent question from parents is how to get their children to go to their room when they are upset so that the rest of the family does not have to be disturbed by their tantrums. In these situations, parents do not want to give attention to their child in the overload phase, and they want to have their child leave the space where the family is gathered, like the dining room or family room. The problem is that children who are extremely angry are not likely to listen to parents' requests to leave the area. And if a parent tries to talk with a child about going to his room, the child is likely to escalate and refuse to leave. The parent could ignore the child and try to carry on with the rest of the family while the child is screaming, but this is sometimes very hard on the rest of the family. How do you watch a movie or eat dinner, while one child is screaming at the top of his lungs?

There are several choices for what you can try. Each choice has some pros and cons. Choice one is let your child scream and the rest of the family try to ignore it, or move the family into another room. The advantage of this approach is that you are not trying to reason with a screaming child who is beyond reason! The disadvantage is that everyone else is inconvenienced. Furthermore, if you move to another room, there is no guarantee that your angry child won't follow you.

Another strategy to consider is developing a back-up consequence that would be applied if your child does not go up to his room when asked. The idea is that the back up consequence would be "worse," or a more severe consequence, than for your child to go to his room. It should be a short term consequence, and should be something you can easily apply later that day. For example, you could take away television or computer privileges for the rest of the day if your child does not go to his room.

A word of warning: you do not want to introduce the back up consequence while your child is having a tantrum. Your child is not thinking rationally then, and he is likely to escalate, or just not consider what you have to say. So if you are going to try this approach, you first want to introduce the idea when everyone is calm. Then the next time your child is getting frustrated, you would cue your child to go to his room when he is starting to get upset, not when he is already in overload. He is more likely to be rational and to heed your request if he is not already in complete overload. If he does not go to his room, then ignore him, and apply the consequence later that day after the tantrum is over.

The advantage of this approach is that most children (if thinking rationally) would rather take a brief time out in their room, rather than suffer a consequence like no television and/or no computer time. The disadvantage of this approach is that your child may escalate again when you impose the consequence. Be sure to stay calm when you mention the consequence, and if your child escalates, remain calm and ignore him. When your child sees you mean business, he may be less likely to escalate in the future and more likely to take his time out to avoid the consequence. This strategy, in other words, may pay off in the long run, even if your child tests you and tries to scream his way out of it the first few times you apply the consequence.

Another idea is to make going to his room fun and relaxing at times that your child is not angry at all. Suggest a fun activity in his room and join him sometimes, or if your child is playing alone in his room, check in on him and make a compliment about what he has been working on. You want the activity in his room to be so enjoyable (and something he can do again and again--like Legos, drawing, or a video game) that your child won't mind your suggestion to go there on a day that he is starting to get upset. Again the key is to suggest it when he is starting to get upset, when he is still thinking rationally. If you wait too long, he will be less likely to listen to you.

Lastly, see if you can anticipate and prevent an upset, rather than try to manage it once your child is already angry. Can you can identify a theme for what is causing some of his tantrums? Then you may be able to head off a tantrum when that issue is about to come up again by making a reassuring comment or suggesting a distracting activity, like a hand held game or drawing. The main difference here from my pervious suggestions in this chapter is that you bring up the distracting activity, or you make a reassuring comment, before your child even starts to get upset because you anticipate that there might be a problem.

Let's say the theme of previous upsets is that your seven year old is jealous because you were interacting (paying attention) to his sibling at dinner. Then the next time the family has dinner, before you start talking with his sibling, you could say to your seven year old something like "now it is your brother's turn to talk, but I will give you a turn in a few minutes." Then compliment him while he is waiting and remind him it will soon be his turn. Try not to wait too long the first few times you try this.

Or suggest your child try an activity while he waits, such as play a hand held game, or draw a picture. Of course, you would have to have these activities on hand and be willing to use them at the dinner table. At some restaurants it is not uncommon for the host to bring a puzzle page or crayons to occupy children while they are waiting for their food. You would be using the same approach at home.

Finally, think about how realistic your expectations are for the length of time you want your child to sit at the table. Young children (and some older children) like to get up and move around while they are eating. If your child is on the active side, or if there is something he is eagerly waiting to do, he may want to leave the table after eating his meal. He may not want to wait for everyone to finish. As parents, think about what your goals are for family dinners, and also consider what is reasonable to expect of your children, given their age and personality.

The question therefore to ask yourself is why does your child have tantrums at the dining table. See if you can come up with a reassuring statement or a distracting activity for him that will head off a tantrum, or consider changing your expectations if you think you may be asking too much of your child. The same suggestions apply if your child tends to have a tantrum during a different family activity, such as family game or television time. As the saying goes, "an ounce of prevention..."

Worksheet for Anger at Meals or Family Activities

What is the situation when your child tends to tantrum?

_____

What is the theme? _____

What are your expectations and are they realistic?

_____

What cue can you use to help your child have a new perspective (or what will be your reassuring words)? _____

If your child starts to get frustrated, what distracting activities will you have available? Or will you ask him to play in his room?

_____

If your child reaches the overload stage, will you ignore him, try to move to another room, or ask him to leave?

_____

If your child reaches the overload stage, will you use a backup consequence later on?

_____

Teasing

Sometimes if your child is teased by peers in school, it is not harmful and can be laughed off, but sometimes it can get mean and hurtful. If you think your child is being overly sensitive, review the earlier chapter in this book about helping sensitive children keep perspective. However, if you think your child is being teased in a hurtful way, I would suggest talking with your child about different reasons that children do this. One possibility is that another child may be jealous of him, and another possibility is that the other child is feeling insecure about something and is trying to make himself feel better by putting someone else down. Ask your child to think about the "teaser" and what his motivation could be. Help him to realize the "teaser" has a problem--jealousy or insecurity. It is also important to empathize with the child that no one likes being teased a lot.

How might your child respond? For minor teasing, you could teach your child to ignore it (give a cold shoulder instead of giving attention to the "teaser"). If it is more serious and takes the form of taunts or harmful insults, ask if your child wants to talk with an adult in school about it, or if he wants you to call the school. You could ask the teacher to speak to the "bully," or keep an eye out to catch him in the act. Another possibility is for the teacher to arrange to have your child's friends (or at least "kind" peers) sit near your child more often in class. Which approach the teacher takes depends in part on what the teacher and your child are comfortable with, and depends on how serious and frequent the teasing is.

If your child wants to try to handle it on his own, one option is for him to tell one of his friends in school and try to sit near him (preferably a big or popular kid) who might help intimidate the "teaser." You might also encourage your child to invite friends to join him at recess or lunch (where most teasing occurs in school).

Think about whether your child feels more confident after your discussion that the teaser is jealous or insecure. Does your child feel he can ignore it or reach out to his peers for help? Or if the teasing is intense and hurtful, you or your child could speak to the teacher or principal to see if an adult at the school can talk to the "teaser" and/or sit your child away from him. For serious teasing, you would explain to your child that the "teaser" has major problems, and it takes many people (the teacher and other students) working together to get through to a child who has major problems.

If your child loses control of his anger when he is teased, I would recommend you try to help your child see how he is viewed by others when he has an explosion in school. Often a child does not realize what effect his tantrums will have on other people's opinions of him. I recommend talking with the child when he is calm and explain that some potentially friendly children may be scared off by his explosions and may avoid playing with him. You could add that some children might get a kick out of seeing him explode. He does not want them to get a laugh at his expense.

While you are pointing out the negative consequences for having angry explosions in school, you also want to be sure to empathize with how difficult it is sometimes to control anger and that you understand how hard it can be not to react to being teased in school. Remember whenever you have a talk about self-control, also be understanding about how hard it can be to avoid an explosion. While it is important to help a child see that angry explosions have a cost, it is also important not to make a child feel worse about himself. You want to motivate your child to work on it with you, but not hurt his self-esteem.

At this point, you could try to teach your child some of the strategies for avoiding anger overload, such as using mantras or other calming techniques. One idea I often suggest to children who are being teased is that they contemplate that one day they may be the teaser's boss and will be able to order the teaser around! I try to help the child "turn the tables" in his mind, if not yet in his everyday life. Refer to my parent's manual for other ways to help your child avoid anger overload.

David Gottlieb, Ph.D.

Violent Cartoons And Video Games

A few parents have written in about violent video games and cartoons. And one parent asked about getting her child a punching bag. Can these activities be a safe outlet, or will they encourage your child to be more violent during an angry outburst? And what do you do if your child gets so upset when he loses a video game that he throws the controller or other objects in the room?

A key idea you want to communicate to your child is that feelings are different from actions. Angry feelings are okay but destructive actions are not. You can explain that anger is a normal emotion, and that while it can be hard to control, it is very important that we work on ways to control it. Punching people or throwing objects that can hurt people or that can be easily broken is not okay. You could then talk about alternative actions that are socially acceptable. For some children, a physical outlet is helpful, while others prefer to talk out their feelings, and still others prefer to distract themselves with music or computer games. I would recommend you try to help your child think of several possible alternatives, and that way when he starts to feel angry, he can choose the one that makes sense to him in a particular situation.

Practicing martial arts or using a punching bag are socially acceptable alternatives. It is okay to let out tension in a physical way so long as no one is hurt. If your child begins to use a punching bag to let out frustrations, I would monitor his behavior over the next month to determine whether there is a change in the frequency of his physically acting out his anger against others. As long as there is not an increase in aggression (and hopefully it helps him with self control and leads to a decrease in anger overload), then continue to allow him to use the punching bag. Maybe he can learn to use it effectively as a tension reliever at home before he gets to the anger overload stage.

Violent cartoons and video games are a favorite of many children. Some studies suggest that violent cartoons do not increase violent behavior of children, and other studies say there can be an increase in aggression for some children, particularly children with poor self control to begin with. If your child has not been overly aggressive towards other people, I would lean toward letting him watch the shows he wants. (Use your judgment though. Some shows can be scary and upsetting for young children.) You might also talk with him sometimes about a cartoon, and discuss why the character reacted the way he/she did.

In video games, the goal is often to eliminate the "boss" at each stage. Some are more graphic than others, and you might discuss with your child how he feels about seeing figures killed in the game. For younger children, you could talk briefly about the difference between fantasy (cartoons and video games) and reality (school), and discuss what he could do if threatened in some way in school or while playing with other children. Recent research suggests children do not become more aggressive if they play violent games, and some studies suggest these games can enhance cognitive skills, like visual motor skills and visual concentration.

I generally suggest parents be aware of what television shows their kids are watching and what video games they are playing. Join them sometimes, because then after the show or game, parents can sometimes talk about the theme of the cartoon or game, and how it might relate (or not relate) to everyday life. Do not overdo the discussions though, or your child may only want to watch her cartoons alone! See how your child reacts, and do not push it if sometimes she does not want to talk.

If your child explodes and throws the game controller at the television when he loses a video game, then consider strategies to help him remain calm. When he has cooled down, talk with your child about how he felt and think together about what else he could do in the future besides throwing things. Help him lower his expectations by explaining that the games are made to make people lose, because if they are too easy people will get bored and stop playing them. Suggest a mantra like "The game is made so that I will win some and lose some." Or, "They make it impossible to win all the time." Practice the mantra together before he starts to play another game. Mention the mantra again each time he wants to play his video games over the next few months. The purpose of repeating the mantra often is so that your child will eventually begin to "hear" it in his head, even when you don't say it.

Another strategy that parents can use is to limit game time to reduce the frequency of upsets. For example, some parents do not allow video games right before bedtime, or limit the time on school days. While this helps somewhat, it is also important to teach your child a coping strategy he can use when he does play the game.

28

Part IV: How To Apply Interventions in School Settings

Many of the strategies in my parent's manual can be applied in school with some modifications to take into account the classroom setting. Let's go through the interventions in part one of the parent's manual first and see where modifications in the strategies need to be made.

Observe patterns:

First, it is important to observe for a couple of weeks, just like in the home, to see what some of the precipitating events are. What was the student doing at the time he got angry, and who, if anyone, was interacting with him/her? Was anything said before he exploded? After writing down your observations for a couple of weeks, you would look over the data to see what patterns, or themes, emerged. You would look for these situations and themes in the future, and whenever possible, intervene early before the anger overload phase.

Prevention:

For example, the situation could be writing an essay during English class, and the issue for your student could be feelings of anxiety about finishing on time. Ideally, you would intervene in a preventive way, before the child even became frustrated. In this example, you could tell the student before the writing assignment, that he/she could have extra time to finish if needed. In this way, you are changing the "demands" of the situation: you are reducing the pressure the child feels to complete his work in a short period of time. While it is impossible to identify every trigger of anger overload for any given child, the goal is to anticipate some of the triggers, and thereby reduce the frequency of anger overload episodes.

In the previous example, the teacher is in essence **changing the child's expectations** that he has to write his essay quickly. Instead, the child knows he can have more time later in the day to finish his essay, so he relaxes. The extra time can be given during a free period or at home. Often the child may not ask for more time, because for a child with anxiety, just knowing he can take the time if he needs it, will help him to relax and write the essay during the regular class period.

Here is another example of how teachers can **change the child's expectations**. If a child tends to get upset when he is not called on in class, you could remind him at the start of the day that you will not be calling on him a lot because you have to give other students a turn. The cue should be a simple sentence to predict what will happen so that the child is not surprised and hopefully not disappointed when you call on other students. In all these situations, the common approach is that you would cue the child before a potentially difficult situation to remind him that things will proceed differently than the way the child has anticipated.

Another common stressor in school is when a child makes mistakes. If this were a trigger, then the teacher would use a cue like "everyone makes mistakes" or "it is good to get some wrong because it means you are learning new things." This cue would be repeated daily so that a child would gradually learn to accept mistakes. Here again you would be trying to change the child's expectations. While this strategy will not work all the time to prevent anger, especially if the child is easily frustrated, over time the child will learn to accept mistakes as a necessary part of learning.

A related strategy that teachers or parents can use is to point out what is positive about the child's school work at the same time that they ask him to correct a mistake. By bringing up what the child has done well, you are helping him keep his mistakes in perspective. The child is less likely to feel hurt and therefore less likely to react with anger.

The other main strategy that is useful in preventing anger arousal is **to change the sequence**. An example here would be to arrange for the child to have time on the computer or to do some other favorite activity following a difficult class assignment. In this way the child has something to look forward to; in a sense there is a reward for doing work that is hard for him. For example, a child may have a weakness in a subject such as reading. The child's schedule could be arranged such that gym, or computer time, would follow reading (assuming the child liked gym). Then he would have something to look forward to after reading.

In a school setting it is not as easy as in the home environment to re-arrange the schedule, though. At home, parents have more flexibility to arrange for something fun to follow a difficult task. It is not always possible in a school setting to have a fun class follow a difficult one because the school schedule involves coordinating the times that various grades use different facilities in the building.

One more suggestion for teachers to consider at the beginning of a school year: It is important early in the school year for the teacher to **build an alliance** with a child prone to anger overload. At home, this alliance has developed with the parents over the years. But in school, the teacher usually changes each year, so that a teacher will need to build rapport at the beginning of the year. Building an alliance will improve the chances that a child will take seriously your interventions. A child will be more likely to use your cues and try to exercise self-control if first a positive rapport has been established. The child will likely trust that you are trying to help and will want to make an effort to please you then. Hopefully you will know ahead of time if a child prone to outbursts will be in your class, and will also know some of the child's interests so that you can discuss these interests with the child to build a bond. Parents can help a teacher learn about their child by planning a meeting with the teacher early in the year, preferably before school even starts.

Early anger phase:

For the early anger phase, ideally there would be a place in the classroom or just outside the room where the child could go if he is getting frustrated. It would not be a punishment but a "chill" space that this child and others could use to decompress. You would assign an activity for this space that would help **distract** the child, or the counseling staff could teach the child a **relaxation strategy** to use there. Depending on the structure of the school, the teacher would decide where this space might be, either in a corner of the room or somewhere outside the class.

Sometimes it will work to ask the child to get up and help you with something. This change can help the child forget about what he has been doing. The advantage of this approach is that you do not have to set up a separate relaxation station for the child. The disadvantage is that not every child who is starting to get angry will respond in a positive way to your request for help. Think about whether this child might be glad that you asked for his help, or whether he is more likely to feel burdened by your suggestion. Some children like to be helpers, and others do not.

For children who quickly get loud when they are frustrated and for children who need more than a few minutes to cool down, a space outside the room might be best, because then the other students in the class would not be disturbed. Also, it will usually be easier for a child to calm down if other students are not watching and commenting on his behavior. A child may continue his angry behavior if he is getting the attention of his classmates, even if it is negative attention.

Now that I have explained the advantages of a space outside the class, let me mention the disadvantages. First a school may not have an extra quiet room that can be utilized for this purpose. In addition, this approach requires an extra teacher or aide to accompany the child to the other space. Lastly, some children may get more agitated if they are asked to leave the room, because this is usually seen as a punishment. Thus, if this approach is to be used effectively, it will be important from the start of the year to communicate to the child the difference between a "chill" space and a punishment. There should be no negative consequences for going to the chill space. In fact, a child should be praised for using the space to calm down.

One other word of caution about using a space outside the classroom: Sometimes a child may try to avoid a difficult assignment by acting up so that he can go to the chill space. If you feel a child is manipulating the system to avoid work, then you could talk with the child later that day and suspend his use of the chill space for a week or more. Before re-instituting this option, you should consider whether the child really needs a place to calm down and whether he can learn to use it only when really necessary.

The other strategy I write about in the parent's manual, **emotional distraction**, will be harder to use in the classroom setting than at home. This strategy involves either

a) making a distracting comment that is silly or in some way changes the child's emotional state, or b) changing the activity to something the child likes to do. In a classroom full of students, a teacher cannot have the child play a fun game whenever he starts to get frustrated. Not only is this impractical but also often counterproductive, since it essentially rewards a child for starting to get angry.

As for using distracting, funny comments, usually the more dramatic an adult's comment, the better it is at changing the child's mood. How does the teacher do this without disrupting the entire class? You could try whispering in a child's ear, or writing a funny message for the child to read at his seat. An example for a child getting frustrated with his work could be "Some days, when I was a kid, I'd rather have a bird crap on me than go to school." Why talk about bird crap? Because children find comments about excrements to be funny. Whether you use words like "crap" depends on the child's age and your school's policies about acceptable language.

For some children you might want to use an empowering message such as: "Your brain is like a super hero's (name one that he likes). Picture the super hero in your mind, and he will help you think of something." The idea is to change the child's mood from frustration and defeat to a feeling of power and success.

Think about what the child's interests are and see if you can think of a phrase or comment that is related to his interests. For example, if a child is interested in Japanese cartoons, you might mention the name of one of the characters, and ask the child to take a moment to summon the character's powers! Or is there a funny saying from the child's favorite cartoon that will bring a smile to his face? It will be easier to employ this strategy if there is an aide in the room who can attend to the child's emotional state and who can be ready to employ a distracting message. Sometimes the teacher or aide may need to try a few different distracting comments before they find one that works for that child.

Overload phase:

While at home a parent can walk away and allow a child to scream, in a classroom this would be too disruptive to the other students. So in school, it will be necessary to have a child in the overload phase leave the classroom. Since the child is not usually thinking rationally at that moment, it is often necessary to have an aide accompany the child, and the child is usually loud and disruptive on the way out of the room.

Where should the child go? I prefer a place at the end of a hallway or a room where noise is not going to be a major disruption to others. The aide would say as little as possible (to avoid giving the child attention) until the child was calmer. If the school office is used, it is important that the secretaries not talk to the child a lot, because this can be reinforcing, and the child may then want to come back to the office for the attention he gets. Another possibility is to use the "chill" space, but sometimes the chill space is in the classroom or another room that has a lot of items that a child in overload might "trash", and in that case the end of the hallway or an empty lunchroom or auditorium might work better. Another problem with using the chill space is that you want the chill space to be seen positively as a "cool" place to relax for a few minutes, rather than be seen as a place for major tantrums. Ultimately, it would be up to the school administrators to decide what would work best in their building.

If a child is going to require physical restraints in order not to harm himself or others (and in order not to destroy property) then an alternative school placement is often necessary. A regular school environment does not usually have the staff or space to handle physically destructive behavior.

When to use rewards and consequences:

This is one strategy where a school often has an advantage over the home. Schools usually have practice using positive and negative reinforcement; for children who often experience anger overload in school, the idea would be to use short term rewards and consequences that they can earn daily. Not only can the rewards be fun to earn, but children get secondary attention later in the day by showing their parents and siblings what they earned in school.

It will be important to connect the rewards and consequences with specific behaviors that have to do with self-control. Explain when the child is calm what behaviors would lead to a reward and what would lead to a brief consequence. Pick incentives and consequences that the child would care about (sometimes it's trial and error to find what works) and that you can employ fairly easily in your classroom.

Think about what a child might be capable of and make the target behavior something that is achievable if the student tries. Over time, you can add to the list of what is expected. This gradual increase in expectations is called "shaping" a behavior.

Let me give you an example of how this principle might be applied in school. An initial behavioral goal might be for the child to follow your instructions to use the chill space to calm down. Another possible behavioral goal could be to avoid certain words, like cursing, when the child is angry. But other behaviors such as arguing with the teacher, or making loud remarks, would not have a consequence at the start. Over time, as the child exhibited better self-control, the teacher might then reward alternatives to loud remarks and arguing.

It is important that besides telling a child what not to do that you also demonstrate acceptable expressions of frustration for inside the classroom. For example, saying "this is really hard" or "I don't like math" is a step toward better control than saying loudly "I hate this" or "school is a pain in the butt." Start where you think the child is capable of making some improvement, and then adjust your expectations over time. I usually suggest waiting until the child achieves the goal eighty per cent of the time over a two to three week period before increasing the expectations.

Additional Strategies for Teachers and Parents

Be a role model:

Just as in the home, adults in school can serve as models for self-control. When a teacher is having a frustrating day, it may be possible to share with the child, or with the whole class, how the teacher might handle this. The remarks could be about something that happened in school or outside of school, but stay away from talking about how frustrating some children in the classroom can be. By way of example, if you had to finish all the report cards, or read the class's essays, by the next school day, you could say "I have so much grading to do tonight I'm not going to have time to watch one of my favorite television shows, but, oh well, I'll just have to work hard tonight and then I can watch all the television I want tomorrow." Children look up to their teachers and parents, so how you handle stress illustrates possibilities for them to emulate!

Here is a worksheet you can use to outline your strategies for one type of situation that triggers your student's anger. An extra copy to use for another trigger is included in the appendix.

Worksheet for Teachers: Developing Strategies for School

Observe patterns:

One situation where there has been anger overload in the last two weeks (What was the activity?):

_____

Who was interacting with the child?_____

What did each person say or do?_____

_____

Were there early signs of frustration in the child's facial expression, tone, verbalizations or behavior? _____

What were the child's expectations?

_____

What, if anything, was expected of the child? _____

(The latter two questions about expectations help you summarize what was underlying the child's upset. It helps you identify one of the child's triggers.)

Prevention:

What will be the altered expectation I'd like to impress upon this child?

_____

What cue words can I use to remind the child of the changed expectations?

_____

Can I alter the routine so that something fun follows a difficult assignment?

_____

Early anger phase:

Possible calming or distracting activities: _____

_____

Will I use a "chill space? _____

Possible funny or empowering comments to change the child's emotion:

_____

Overload phase:

What will be the plan if the child reaches the overload phase?

_____

Using rewards and consequences:

Will I use incentives (in addition to praise)? _____

What behaviors or words would earn an incentive? _____

Will I use a consequence? _____

What behaviors or words would trigger a consequence?

_____

Teaching your student cognitive skills:

Most of the cognitive strategies require individual discussions with the child, and could be part of a treatment plan for the school social worker or counselor. These suggestions usually work better with children who are in the third grade or older. The child needs to have some ability to look at his behavior: to recognize that he was out of control and to want to change that. If a child is only blaming others or denies he has a problem, I'd recommend the school focus on the previous suggestions that can be used by teachers without a child's direct participation.

The counselor may want to coordinate his approach with the parents, so that if a child is having outbursts at home as well, the counselor could work on the same steps in school that the parents are working on at home. Self-control is not easy for children prone to anger overload, so that repetition of strategies at home and at school will help reinforce a new approach for dealing with anger.

In terms of scheduling time for the child to meet with the school counselor or social worker, I find it is usually better to have two brief, ten to fifteen minute, sessions a week, rather than one longer session. It will also be important for the classroom teacher to communicate ahead of time with the social worker what angry behavior was observed in the classroom. If the counselor meets twice a week with the student, there is a good chance that some of the meetings will coincide with a day the child has misbehaved. It is more likely that a child will remember his behavior and be willing to work on it, if a whole week hasn't gone by since an incident.

If the child does not remember everything that the teacher noted about his behavior, it is okay if the child can acknowledge some part of what happened and work on alternatives. The goal is not to have the child accept everything he said or did when he was angry, but to work on strategies to begin to deal with his anger.

It will be important for the counselor to communicate back with the teacher about the plan. If the counselor is teaching a calming strategy for example, and the teacher knows what it is, then the teacher can cue the child to try it at the appropriate time, when the child is starting to get frustrated.

The school may want to keep the parents abreast weekly of what was worked on so that the parents can praise the child for his efforts. If the child was able to maintain self-control some of the days of the week, the parents could talk that up at home. In other words, focus on the positives at home, rather than criticize the child for losing control. If parents were to talk mainly about times the child did not control himself, the child might be less cooperative with the skills training at school, and be less likely to talk over his experiences at home in the future.

Part V: Finding Professional Help:

If you are having difficulty applying the strategies at home, or if you have tried for a few months and there is little or no progress, it may be helpful to get a consult from a mental health professional. A mental health professional can help you decide if there are other issues interfering with progress, and can help you implement the strategies if you are feeling stuck. How do you search for someone who has experience with anger issues in children?

Anger overload is a term I coined to capture the problem that some children have with anger. These children react quickly and intensely to frustration or disappointment. Professionals in your area may not use the term "anger overload." What you want to know from the professional is not what words they use to describe the problem, but whether they have experience in helping children who have intense angry outbursts. Ask a potential counselor whether he/she has dealt with anger issues in children and what his approach is.

I believe it is best when the therapist works with parents as well as the child. Since most children will not use strategies on their own, it is important for the therapist to work with parents, who can then implement the strategies at home. If the therapist wants to do individual therapy with the child and does not plan to meet often with the parents, ask why. If the child is suffering from some other condition like trauma, individual therapy may be indicated. But for many children with anger overload, I find individual therapy to be less effective than including the parents in the treatment plan.

The therapist may prefer to work with the parents separately or meet with everyone together. How often the child is included in the sessions will depend in part on how open he is to discussing the issues without feeling criticized or hurt. Also it will depend on which part of the manual (which strategy) you are working on. If you are working on the strategies in the second half of my manual, such as learning about other points of view and learning how to compromise, it would be helpful to have the child participate in joint sessions with the parents. Your child's input then is important in working through the strategy. If your child is not working on these strategies yet, then the therapist may choose to meet with your child in the beginning to get a good diagnostic impression, and then strategize more often with you alone. The strategies in the first half of the manual are implemented by the parents and do not require the child's direct participation.

When you try strategies at home, the therapist will be able to guide you and help you make modifications for your child. Sometimes it is hard to see what is causing the problem because you are emotionally involved in the situation. It can help to have the input of a neutral observer. Also, some children respond better to one strategy or set of strategies than to others, and a therapist can help you decide whether to continue to work on a strategy despite a child's resistance or whether it is better to change to a different strategy.

Therapists who work with children and families can have different academic degrees. Some will have a masters in counseling or social work, and others will have a doctorate in psychology or psychiatry. The key is whether a) they work primarily with children and their families and whether b) they have experience helping children with anger problems. You might show them my manual or my blog, and ask whether these issues are something they are familiar with. They may not follow my manual exactly, but use some similar techniques.

To find someone in your area, you might ask your child's doctor or teacher who they recommend. Also, some state psychological associations and social work associations offer a referral service. You can find out who in your area works with children and families, and then contact potential therapists to ask whether they have worked on anger issues. You can meet with a few therapists if you are unsure who to work with, and then choose the therapist who makes the most sense to you.

If your child potentially has a co-occurring condition like bipolar disorder or ADHD, then a psychiatrist can he helpful with medication for the co-occurring condition. If you treat the co-existing diagnosis, it will be easier to work on the anger issues with your child. Once any mood or attention elements are under better control with the medication, then the child will be able to focus more on strategies to deal with his anger. If you are unsure if your child has a co-occurring condition, check with a mental health professional in your area (either psychiatrist, psychologist or social worker) for a diagnostic evaluation. You can also learn about possible diagnoses on your own before meeting with a professional. For example, I have written about co-occurring problems in an earlier book called "Your Child Is Defiant: Why Is Nothing Working?"

Appendix: Worksheets

Worksheet for Helping Sensitive Children

What trigger will you help your child deal with?

_____

What will be the cue to help your child keep perspective?

_____

Will you use a picture, song, or jingle to help reinforce the cue words?

_____

Is there an example from your own life you can mention as a model for your child?

_____

Additional Strategies for Teachers and Parents

Worksheet for Incentives and Consequences

Which anger trigger will you be working on? _____

What coping strategy do you want your child to try?

_____

What cue words will you use to remind him if he starts to get frustrated?

_____

What incentives can your child choose from if he tries?

_____

What specific behavior will lead to a negative consequence?

_____

What will be the brief negative consequence?

_____

Worksheet for Creating Stories and Jingles

What trigger will you focus on?

_____

What characters and activity in your story will capture the trigger in a dramatic way?

_____

Will you use puppets or toy figures to tell your story?

_____

Will you use a jingle or song?

_____

What alternative behavior(s) do you wish your child would use?

_____

How will you resolve your story in a way that suggests an alternative?

_____

Additional Strategies for Teachers and Parents

Worksheet for Anger at Meals or Family Activities

What is the situation when your child tends to tantrum?

_____

What is the theme? _____

What are your expectations, and are they realistic?

_____

What cue can you use to help your child have a new perspective (or what will be your reassuring words)? _____

If your child starts to get frustrated, what distracting activities will you have available? Or will you ask him to play in his room?

_____

If your child reaches the overload stage, will you ignore him, try to move to another room, or ask him to leave?

_____

If your child reaches the overload stage, will you use a backup consequence later on?

_____

Worksheet for Teachers: Developing Strategies for School

Observe patterns:

One situation where there has been anger overload in the last two weeks (What was the activity?):

_____

Who was interacting with the child?_____

What did each person say or do?_____

_____

Were there early signs of frustration in the child's facial expression, tone, verbalizations or behavior? _____

What was the child's expectations?

_____

What, if anything, was expected of the child?_____

Prevention:

What will be the altered expectation I'd like to impress upon this child?

_____

What cue words can I use to remind the child of the changed expectations?

_____

Can I alter the routine so that something fun follows a difficult assignment?

_____

Early anger phase:

Possible calming or distracting activities:

_____

Will I use a "chill space? _____

Possible funny or empowering comments to change the child's emotion:

_____

Additional Strategies for Teachers and Parents

Overload phase:

What will be the plan if the child reaches the overload phase?

_____

Using rewards and consequences:

Will I use incentives (in addition to praise)? _____

What behaviors or words would earn an incentive? _____

Will I use a consequence? _____

What behaviors or words would trigger a consequence?

_____

Made in the USA
Lexington, KY
21 February 2016